# My Very First
# CHRISTMAS

D0166951

Written by Juliet David
Illustrations by Helen Prole

Copyright © 2016 Lion Hudson/Tim Dowley Associates Ltd

Published by Candle Books
an imprint of
**Lion Hudson plc**
Wilkinson House, Jordan Hill Road,
Oxford OX2 8DR, England
www.lionhudson.com/candle

ISBN 978 1 78128 2854
e-ISBN 978 1 78128 314 1

First edition 2016
Taken from *Baby Jesus is Born*, first published 2007

A catalogue record for this book is available from the British Library

Printed and bound in China, June 2016, LH17

# My Very First
# CHRISTMAS

Juliet David
Illustrated by Helen Prole

CANDLE
BOOKS

In a little town called Nazareth there lived a young woman named Mary.

Mary was engaged to a man named Joseph.
He was the town carpenter.

One day an angel appeared.
"Mary!" he said. "You are going to have a very special baby. You must name him Jesus."

Mary was so very happy.
She made up a special song to thank God.

Mary and Joseph soon got married.
They were looking forward to the arrival
of Mary's baby.

But Joseph had to go back to his home town, Bethlehem, to be counted. Mary and Joseph made the long journey together.

At last they saw the town in the distance.
Night was falling. They still needed
to find somewhere to sleep.

Bethlehem was full of people.
"I have no room!" said the innkeeper.
"But you could stay in my stable." So they did.

That night, baby Jesus was born
in the innkeeper's stable.
Mary wrapped him in warm cloths.
Joseph tucked him in the animals' manger.

In fields nearby, shepherds
were guarding their sheep.

All of a sudden, an angel appeared.

"Don't be scared!" he said.
"A baby is born in Bethlehem.
One day he will save the world!"

Then a whole crowd of angels started to sing.

After they had finished, the shepherds raced off
into Bethlehem to find this special baby.

Soon the shepherds found baby Jesus.
They knelt down before him.
Mary felt very happy.

Far away, some wise men were watching the skies. Suddenly they saw a new star. "This means a great king is born!" said one.

So the wise men decided to follow the star.
They journeyed across deserts and mountains.
They believed the star would lead
them to the newborn baby.

After many days and nights, the star
did lead the wise men to Bethlehem.
There they found baby Jesus.

The wise men had brought with them
rich presents for the baby king.

They gave little Jesus shiny gold, and costly perfumes called frankincense and myrrh.

That night an angel warned Joseph in a dream.
"A wicked king wants to kill baby Jesus.
You must leave at once!"

So Mary, Joseph, and baby Jesus fled
in the night. They escaped to Egypt.

When it was safe, they journeyed back
to Nazareth. There Jesus grew up.
God was preparing him for a very special job.